RABINDRANATH TAGORE

RABINDRANATH TAGORE

The Poet Sublime

Reeta Dutta Gupta

Revised Edition

RUPA

Published by
Rupa Publications India Pvt. Ltd. 2015
7/16, Ansari Road, Daryaganj
New Delhi 110002

Sales centres:
Allahabad Bengaluru Chennai
Hyderabad Jaipur Kathmandu
Kolkata Mumbai

Edition copyright © Rupa Publications India Pvt. Ltd. 2002, 2015

Text copyright © Reeta Dutta Gupta 2002, 2015

All rights reserved.
No part of this publication may be reproduced, transmitted,
or stored in a retrieval system, in any form or by any means, electronic,
mechanical, photocopying, recording or otherwise, without the prior
permission of the publisher.

The views and opinions expressed in this book are the author's own and
the facts are as reported by her which have been verified to the extent
possible, and the publishers are not in any way liable for the same.

ISBN: 978-81-291-3668-8

First impression 2015

10 9 8 7 6 5 4 3 2 1

The moral right of the author has been asserted.

Typeset by Ninestars Information Technologies Ltd, Chennai

Printed at : Aarvee Printers Pvt. Ltd. New Delhi

This book is sold subject to the condition that it shall not, by way
of trade or otherwise, be lent, resold, hired out, or otherwise
circulated, without the publisher's prior consent, in any form
of binding or cover other than that in which it is published.

This book is for Cara

CONTENTS

Chapter One: Life and Times 9

Chapter Two: Tagore and His Works 28

Chapter Three: Tagore the Nobel Laureate 58

Chapter Four: Tagore the Musician and the Painter ... 66

From the *Gitanjali* 74

Chronology 78

Bibliography 81

CHAPTER ONE

LIFE AND TIMES

Many glowing tributes have been paid to Rabindranath Tagore, but one that surely touches the heart was by the mother of the English war-poet Wilfred Owen, who was killed only a week before the war was over. She wrote to Tagore to tell him that when her son came to bid goodbye and they looked across a sun-drenched sea with breaking hearts, her poet-son had recited 'those wonderful words of yours':

> *When I go from hence, let this be my parting word,*
> *that what I have seen is unsurpassable.*
> *I have tasted of the hidden honey of this lotus that*
> *expands on the ocean of light, and thus am I blessed—*
> *let this be my parting word.*

10 • RABINDRANATH TAGORE

*'Singing to my Father',
The young Rabindranath with
Maharshi Debendranath,
painting by Gaganendranath
Tagore, 1911*

And she continued, 'when his pocket book came back to me—I found these words written in his dear writing—with your name beneath. Would it be asking too much of you, to tell me what book I should find the whole poem?'

A poet, musician, dramatist, novelist, painter, and an educator, Rabindranath Tagore (1861–1941), the literar genius of Bengal, attained international fame. He has been widely acclaimed as India's greatest poet of his age. His multifaceted creative intellect manifested itself in a wide variety of literary *genres* and he expressed himself in lyrics, sonnets, songs, prose-poems, poetic narratives, nonsense verse, dance-drama, short stories, novels, plays, essays on religion, philosophy and aesthetics. The vast range and variety of his work collected in 30 heavy volumes (and is still being collected) is amazing.

In 1913 Tagore won the Nobel Prize for Literature for his exquisite collection of mystical hymns *Gitanjali* (Songs

Offerings). In 1915 he was awarded the knighthood, but he surrendered it in 1919 in protest against General Reginald Dyer's Jallianwalla Bagh massacre at Amritsar. In 1940, a year before his death, the Oxford University held a special convocation at Santiniketan, the school he founded outside Calcutta near Bolpur. It conferred on Tagore, who had given up school at the age of fourteen but was 'Most dear to all Muses,' the Doctorate degree for Literature.

Son of Maharishi Debendranath Tagore and Sarada Devi, Rabindranath Tagore (Rabi Thakur of the Bengalis) was born to wealth and affluence on 7 May 1861, in the aristocratic family mansion of Jorasanko, in Calcutta. Tagore's grandfather, Dwarkanath (1794–1846), an elite business magnate, known for his magnanimity, had helped in the development of the city's pioneer institutions like the Hindu College and the Calcutta Medical College.

Tagore at the age of twelve

Rabindranath Tagore, around the age of 17 in England

A friend of Raja Rammohan Roy (1772–1833), who founded the Brahmo Samaj that spearheaded the movement for purging the Hindu way of life of its many evils, Dwarkanath was most progressive in his outlook. European paintings and western furnitures, and garden parties with splendid dinners, drinking and dancing were all part of his lifestyle. He had acquired estates in the Padma river region in north-east Bengal, now in Bangladesh. Here in Shelidah, the estate office, Tagore often living in a house boat was to pen several of his masterpieces in the 1890s.

Tagore was born at the dawn of a new age in Bengal, when socio-religious movements gained momentum denouncing age-old evils like bigotry, inequalities, and superstitions. Iswar Chandra Vidyasagar (1820–1891) and others advocated widow remarriage, abolition of child marriage and woman's education. And in Bengali literature, Michael Madhusudan Dutta (1824–73) with his epic poetry, Dinabandhu Mitra (1829–74) with his protest play against the exploitation of Indigo planters, Bankim Chandra Chatterji (1838–94), the foremost novelist, and the poet Biharilal Chakravarti (1824–73) had all made their impact. Tagore observed, 'When I came on the scene... the new age had just declared itself... .'

Tagore's father, Debendranath (1817–1905), a scholar of Sanskrit, Persian, Indian and Western Philosophy,

14 • RABINDRANATH TAGORE

Jorasanko, home of the Tagores

became a Brahmo in 1843. A spiritual experience made him turn inwards and he often sought the silence and solitude of the high Himalayas and became known as *Maharshi*, the great sage. Tagore is said to have often turned to his father's compilation *Brahmo Dharma*, with excerpts from the Indian scriptures, for constant spiritual inspiration. In 1873 he took along with him his son, Rabi, the child Rabindranath, on his first trip to the mountains. From Calcutta they went to Santineketan (Tagore's first visit), where his father had bought a piece of land in 1863, and then via Amritsar, they reached the hill station of Dalhousie. Here, he had his first taste of freedom as his father let him roam the hillside freely.

The last scene of Post Office *being staged at Jorasanko, 1917. Rabindranath Tagore is seen second from right*

Glad not to go to school, which he found boring and agonizing, he later wrote, 'The Bengal Academy (his school) and the Himalaya—oh, the difference!' Later, throughout his life, the poet was always on the move, travelling to Ahmedabad, Bombay, Chandernagore, Sholapur, Poona, Ghazipur, Madras, Pondicherry and to the hills—Almora, Darjeeling, Kalimpong, Mungpoo—and crossing continents, and changing abodes.

Tagore was the fourteenth and the youngest child. His sister Saudamini looked after him when an infant, while his mother remained busy with her large household. As a boy, he was relegated to the care of servants, who often confined him within a chalk-circle in a room. In his memoir, Tagore tells us how from his confinement he would look out from his window for hours at a pond with a banyan tree on one side and a coconut grove on the other. And how as a child he felt that both life and the world filled with mystery—'It was as if Nature shut her hands and laughingly asked, "What have I got inside?" and nothing seemed impossible.'

The Jorasanko house was full of children and before going off to bed, Rabi and others gathered in the glow of lamps to listen to folklore told by the servants. One of them, a former village schoolmaster, recited stories from the *Ramayana* and the *Mahabbarata*. And though he went to a number of schools—Oriental Seminary, Normal School, Bengal Academy, St Xaviers—it was home tuitions that gave Rabi a solid grounding in Bengali, Sanskrit, English and basic Science. Apart from mathematics, history, geography, etc. he was given lessons in wrestling, music, drawing, and gymnastics. His attendance at school suffered seriously and he was withdrawn from school in 1875. Later, in 1878, when he was sent to the University College, London, to study law, he returned to India within a year sans a degree. But Tagore was a voracious reader and with a tutor he had read Kalidasa's *Kumarasambhava* and Shakespeare's *Macbeth* in the original, and was made to render these in Bengali.

Tagore grew up in a highly gifted family and in a rich literary and cultural ambience. Almost every member of the family was involved in literary, dramatic, musical or artistic activities. As a child Rabi memorized passages from his eldest brother, Dwijendranath's composition *Svapnaprayan* (Dream journey), just by listening to it, which left a deep impression on him. In his brother's library was a collection of Vaishnava lyrics, the early religious lyrics of Bengal, of which he was very fond as he was of the rhythmic poetry of Jayadeva's *Geeta Govinda*. Critics have noted the influence of the Vaishnava lyrics and the Upanishads on Tagore's work. He was closest to Dwijendranath, and another brother, the versatile musician, poet, dramatist, artist Jyotirindranath and his wife, Kadambari Devi, they ran a literary club that was attended by the elite intellectuals of the city. Tagore's second brother, Satyendranath, Tagore, was the first Indian member of the Indian Civil Service, and his wife Jnanadanandini started the children's magazine *Balak* for which Tagore wrote regularly as he did for *Bharati*, the family magazine.

On 9 December 1883 Tagore was married to Mrinalini Devi Raichaudhuri, then only a girl, who bore him three daughters: Madhurilata (Bela), Renuka (Rani), and Mira (Atasi), and two sons: Rathindranath and Shamindra. Six months after his marriage, in 1884, his sister-in-law

With his wife, Mrinalini Devi

Kadambari Devi, friend and inspiration, who was a little older than him and whose touch he felt 'in every aspect of my being,' committed suicide. He had lost his mother when he was thirteen, but this was 'the first great sorrow of his life.' And yet, 'in the midst of this suffocating darkness,' Tagore felt 'there would suddenly blow over my heart, now and again, a breeze of gladness, taking me by surprise.' For life had to move on...

In 1889 Tagore's father transferred the management of their family estates in East Bengal from son Jyotirindranath to Rabindranath. It was here, and earlier in Chandernagore, that Tagore came into close contact with Bengal's beautiful riverine countryside, and as Krishna Kripalani says, the spell of Bengal's river-life 'runs through his poetry like the murmur of a lullaby.' Here too he came into contact with the peasant folk, for whom he always felt great empathy and tenderness.

In 1901 Tagore founded a boarding-school-cum-ashram, Brahmacharya A shram, at Santineketan. Here he attempted to bring together the best of Indian and Western traditions of philosophy with the aim of creating a unique education system. A system that was close to nature and which valued space and freedom, which he loved so much and which he believed was indispensable for a child's total development. Here, initially, Tagore took classes, corrected exercise books, and even wrote out

20 • RABINDRANATH TAGORE

textbooks. And though he travelled a lot, he was always happy to return to Santineketan, the 'abode of peace.' Tagore's numerous essays on education stressed the need for woman's education and pleaded for instruction through the mother tongue. In 1921 the Visva-Bharati University was founded at Santineketan. It was at Santineketan that Tagore began to be called Gurudev, the great teacher.

In his own lifetime, Tagore lost his wife in 1902; his daughter Renuka in 1903; and his youngest son Shamindra in 1907, who died of cholera and for whom he felt a special affection. His father too passed away in 1905, and many years later he lost his daughter Bela, two of his brothers and his only grandson Nitindra. Loss and pain found sublime expression in his poems and not self-pity, and he said sorrow made his lyre sing. For he was

Rabindranath Tagore with his eldest daughter, Madhurilata and son, Rathindranath, 1890

intensely aware of life moving silently forever, renewing itself through death. And so he wrote of the varied game of life on this earth, 'its meetings and partings, its laughter and tears.'

Tagore visited England and the United States several times and he travelled extensively in Europe through France, Holland, Switzerland, Germany, Sweden, Hungary, Austria, Italy, Czechoslovakia and Russia, meeting some of the finest minds of the West—YB Yates, Ezra Pound, Romain Rolland who was impressed by Tagore's lectures on Nationalism, Hellen Keller, the renowned scientist Einstein, Bertrand Russell, Bernard Shaw and Charles Freer Andrews, who became his lifelong friend. In Stockholm he was received by King Gustavus V, and in Germany, a local paper reported,

Open-air classes at Santiniketan

'Scenes of frenzied hero-worship marked a public lecture... In the rush for seats many girls fainted.' He also visited South America, China and Japan, the Far East, South-East Asia, Ceylon (now Sri Lanka), Iran and Iraq. Many of his trips were lecture tours for raising funds for his school. His numerous lectures, travel accounts and letters have been published in several volumes.

Tagore denounced war and rule by force as a mockery of civilization. In a humorous poem *Shradho* he says:

'There, the radio blares threats of the man with the butterfly moustache. In country after country, in towns and villages throats are slit in a frenzy. Who knows who

At a reception given to the Mahatma and Kasturba by the poet at Santiniketan, 1940

shall be victorious as the machine-gun smashes to rubble the foundation of civilization.'

Throughout his life, Tagore spoke against the wrongs of humanity wherever perpetrated. 'And yet,' he said, 'I shall not commit the grievous sin of losing faith in Man.' He believed no storm or tornado could blot out the lamp of love in the human heart, which was the foundation of all religions. Tagore, as Krishna Kripalani says, was 'first and last and above all else a lover.' He was forever in love with life and this earth, and his love for nature and children were two sources of unfailing joy. Once, planting a tree in Hungary, he wrote the following lines, which were later inscribed on a stone:

When I am no longer on this earth, my tree,
Let the ever-renewed leaves of thy spring
Murmur to the wayfarers,
The poet did love while he lived.'

In his concern for rural community development, Tagore was like Mahatma Gandhi with whom he shared a warm friendship despite some serious differences of belief . He hated foreign rule, but he later distanced himself from politics, retiring to Santineketan to sing for his Muse. Having imbibed both Western values as much as the wisdom of India's past, Tagore believed that 'a single heart beats in the breast of mankind.' He stood

24 • RABINDRANATH TAGORE

The poet and the idealist with Jawaharlal Nehru

for the universal man, whose 'world has not been broken up into fragments by narrow domestic wall.' For he believed:

> *When one knows thee, then alien there is none, then no door is shut. Oh, grant me my prayer that I may never lose the bliss of the touch of the one in the play of the many.*
> (*LXIII*Gitanjali)

A humanist and an idealist, Tagore continued to write till the end of his life. Forever experimenting and innovating new forms, new rhythm, he even took to painting at the age of 67, exhibiting his art in the world's

Rabindranath Tagore in the role of Valmiki in the play Valmiki Prativa, *1881*

capital cities. And he was always thankful for the many gifts he had received:

> *Thy infinite gifts come to me only on these very*
> *small hands of mine. Ages pass, and still thou pourest,*
> *and still there is room to fill.*
> (*I*Gitanjali)

Following a period of illness and failing to recover from a surgery, Tagore died in Calcutta on 7 August 1941. But before he was taken to the operating theatre, he dictated his last poem. In a life spanning 80 years, he had accomplished so much, and yet, in the last year of his life, he wrote with his characteristic zest for life in the poem
Oikatan from *Janmadine*:

> *Bipul eh prithivir katotuku jani!*
> *Deshe deshe kato-na nagar rajdhani—*
> *manusher kato kirti, kato nadi giri sindhu maru*
> *Kato-na ajana jib, kato-na aparichito taru*
> *raey gelo agochare.*

(How little I know of this wide world! So many cities and capitals in country after country - how many human achievements, how many rivers, hills, oceans and deserts, how many strange creatures, unfamiliar trees still remain beyond the grasp of my knowledge!)

But the poet was certain that his poetry would live through the ages:

Aji hote sata barsho pare
Ke tumi poricho boshi amar kabita khani
Kautualbhore,
(*from* Chitra)

(A hundred years from now, who are you reading my poem with such curiosity?)

CHAPTER TWO

TAGORE AND HIS WORKS

Rabindranath Tagore wrote 'in many moods of mind' and on a wide range of subjects—love, nature, social, mystical, legendary and historical themes—and in almost every literary *genre* poetry, fiction, drama, essay and criticism. In poetry he wrote romantic narratives, lyrics and sonnets, prose-poems, quatrains, verses for children, and numerous songs. Many of his poems have become immortal for their profundity, lilting rhythm and beauty reflected in thoughts, feelings, language and form. Writing for nearly six decades, Tagore produced an extensive body of work.

Tagore's Poems

Tagore was foremost a poet—and a romantic to the core of his heart. In a letter he said, 'The joy of writing one

poem far exceeds that of writing sheaves and sheaves of prose... If I could only write one poem a day...' Well, he wrote over three thousand poems published in about a hundred collections.
Sanchayita (1931) is his most popular anthology of poems and songs selected by the poet himself.

Tagore wrote his first verse at the age of eight. In 1877 he began to make regular contributions to *Bharati*, the family magazine. In 1882 his *Sandhya Sangit* (Evening Songs), full of 'sadness and pain', written after his first visit to England, drew praises from Bankim Chandra Chatterji, then the leading novelist of Bengal. He is said to have offered his garland to Tagore at a wedding reception. In 1883 came *Prabhat Sangit* (Morning Songs) and the poem *Nirjharer Svapnabhanga* (The Awakening of the Waterfall) from this collection is said 'to mark symbolically the beginning of his adult career as a poet.' Dispelling the earlier gloom, the poet here celebrated a mood of exaltation following a sudden spiritual awakening that lasted for four days, when life appeared bathed in light and glory. *Chhabi O Gan* (Picture and

Song) and *Kadi O Komal* (Sharps and Flats) are works belonging to this early period, but his characteristic love for life and people had found clear expression:

> *Morite chahina ami sundara bhuvane*
> *manober majhe ami banchibare chai.*
> *Aei surjokare aei pushpito kanane*
> *jibanto hriday-majhe jadi sthan pai*
> (*Pran* from *Kari O Komal*)

(I do not wish to die in this beautiful earth, I wish to live among humans. In this sunshine and blooming garden, and at the centre of a loving heart.)

It was with the publication of *Manasi* (Of Mind) in 1890, described as Tagore's first 'book of genius,' containing poems like *Bodhu* (Bride), *Meghdut*, *Ananta Prem* (Unending love), and his second book *Sonar Tari* (1893), containing poems like, *Sonar Tari* (Golden boat), *Dui Pakhi* (Two birds), *Jete Nabi Dibo* (Will not let you go), *Gan Bhango* (Broken Song), and *Vasundhara* (Earth) that Tagore put his golden stamp on Bengali poetry of that period. This was the time when he came into contact with Bengal's countryside. And between 1894 to 1900, he published several of his major books of verses as well as dramas and stories. Some of these collections are: *Chitra, Chaitali* ; *Kanika* (Trifles), which contains four line verses full of wit and wisdom; *Katha* (Ballads), *Kahini* (Tales and legend), *Kalpana* (Dream), and *Ksnanika* (Momentary), of which Kripalani says, 'Tagore never wrote anything finer...than the book of poems with which he closed the fortieth year of his life.' Some of the memorable poems from these collections are: *Puratan Bhritya*, a poem about an old servant who while caring for his sick master dies of small-pox, *Jibandebota*, addressed to Tagore's poetic deity/ inner self, and Sindhu Pare from *Chitra; Didi* (about a girl washing pots on the river bank while her brother hovers around), *Parichay* (about a girl showering love on her brother as well as on a bleating goat), *Meghdut*, from *Chaitali*. The collections *Katha* and *Kahini* contain masterpieces of longer narrative verses like *Debotar-gras, Abhisar, Pujarini, Hari Khela*, and *Gandharir Abedon*, in which Tagore's combined genius as the poet, dramatist and story-teller finds full expression.

Between 1901 to 1929 Tagore wrote *Naivedya* (Offerings), which are sombre religious poems of the highest order; *Smaran* (Remembrance), written in memory of his wife; *Sisu* (Child), which has poems on children; *Kheya* (Crossings), *Gitanjali* (Song Offerings), *Gitimalya* and *Gitali*, which contain ethereal and mystical hymns of devotion; *Balaka* (Swans), which has several of his finest poems like *Sankha* (Conch), *Chhabi* (Picture), *Shajahan, Dan* (Gift), etc; *Palataka* (Fugitive), which has tales in verse and the lovely poem *Thakurdadar*

Chutti (Grandfather's holiday); *Sisu Bholanath*, which has poems on children that were written after the poet detached himself from political involvement and retired to Santineketan; and *Mahua*, which contains several love poems.

In the last decade of his life in the 1930s, Tagore wrote contemplative poems, prose-poems and poems spurred by illness and recovery, but full-flavored with wisdom. He thought *Parisesh* (End) would be his last collection but it was followed by *Punascha* (Postcript), which was dedicated to his grandson, Nitu, who had died prematurely. Some of the other books of verses of this period are: *Bithika* (Avenue), *Patraput* (Plate of Leaves), *Khapchhara* (Non-sense Rhymes), *Prantik* (Borderland), which recorded the poet's experience when he became unconscious and seriously ill in. 1937; *Akash-pradip* (Lamp in the Sky). Between 1940–41 in the last two years of his life came *Navajatak* (New-born), *Rogasajyay* (Sick-bed); *Arogya* (Recovery) written while recovering from an illness, *Janmadine* (On Birthday).

True to his muse, Tagore wrote even in his last hours. Only a week before he died, on 29 and 30 July 1941, he dictated from his bedside his last poems *Dukher Adhar Ratri* and *Tomar Sristir Path*. In his hands Bengali poetry was enriched as never before. Today, after over half a century of his death, Tagores readers will instantly recall and recite from memory stanza after stanza from his poetry:

> *Aji eh prabhate rabir kar*
> *kamone pashilo praner par,*
> *kamone pashilo guhar andhare prabhatpakbir gan!*
> *(Nirjharer Svapnabhanga)*

(How has this morning's sunshine entered into my heart and how has the early morning bird began to sing, penetrating the darkness of the cave?)
And:

> *Where the mind is without fear and the head is held high;*
> *Where knowledge is free,*
> *Where the mind is led forward by thee into ever widening thought*
> *Into that heaven of freedom, my Father, let my country awake.*

(*XXXV*Gitanjali)

Tagore's vast and varied poetry celebrated the longings of the human heart, nature in its calm and destructive form, the idyllic countryside of Bengal, the cyclic roll of seasons, and the lives of the ordinary men, women, and children. His poems are always full of nature, filled with the fragrance of jasmine, champakas, nim and mango blossoms and the roar of the rain clouds—*gagane garaje megh*. He loved the sun. He loved to describe the rains and also the shrubs and trees : *'unripe mangoes dangle from branches* and *a single kurci-tree seems surprised/ by its excess of flowers,'* And he wrote about the beautiful countryside of Bengal, of her blue sky, golden fields of paddy, deep ponds, dancing rivers, and waves running wild:

Nomonomo nomo, sundari momo janani Bangobhumi!
Gan gar tir, snigdha samir, jiban jurale tumi.
Abarita maath, gagan lalat chume taba padadhuli—
Chayasunibir shantir nir chhoto chhoto gram guli

(I bow to you, my beautiful motherland Bengal; to your riverbank and sweet wind that cool and refresh me; to your open plains kissed by the sky; and many little shaded villages with huts filled with peace.)

The metaphor of the changing seasons is a recurrent theme in Tagore's poetry as a symbol of nature's ever-changing mood—the rhythm of flowering and withering, growth and decay. Both in prose and in poetry, he expressed a steady consciousness of this rhythm, of the duality and the coexistence of the opposites in the universe—the infinite and the finite, life and death, joy and sorrow, beauty and decay—that make up the totality of reality. In his poem *Prithvi* (Earth) from *Patraput*, Tagore pays his homage to the earth, which is filled with the silence of the mountains as much as with the noise of sea-waves and is both gentle and fierce, ancient and renewing:

Shubbey-ashubhey-sthapita tomar padopithay
Tomar prochondo sundar mohimar uddeshay
Aaj rakhey jabo amar khatochinhalanchito jibaner pronoti

(Good and evil form at your feet; at your vastly beautiful and terrifying existence, I offer today my life's wounded obeisance.)

Addressing the earth, he says: '*You are beauty and abundance, terror and famine*'. On the one hand, there are '*acres of crops, bent with ripeness*' and on the other hand, '*in your dry, barren, sickly deserts/ The dance of ghosts amid strewn animal-bones*'. But he was full of love for the earth. In his poem *Vasundhara* (Earth), he expressed his intense love for the earth—for the sights, sounds, smells - against the changing background

Tagore in England, 1890

of growth and decay. For Tagore saw Creation, despite its contradictions and conflicts, its impersonality, as supremely beautiful, expressing a divine rhythm that held him spellbound. In a poem in *Rogasajyay*, written in his last years, he says that though there may be in life *grace and ugliness'*, he as a poet was enchanted by *'the huge harmonious beauty'* of the universe that never breaks its rhythm. And everywhere he heard *'His silent footsteps'* so that all the notes of his songs proclaimed:

He comes, comes, ever comes.
Every moment and every age, every day and every
night he comes, comes, ever comes.
(*XLV*Gitanjail)

Repeatedly, Tagore expressed an attitude of gratitude and acceptance of life. Incessantly, he sought the Divine and longed for beauty. As he said, 'I'm a thirst for the beyond,' and his poems reached out for the great unknown. And yet, he remained well rooted to mother earth; like a tree, a river, he kept close to the ground. As in his delightful poem *Tal-gach* (Palm Tree) from *Sisu Bholanath*, so popular with children, which *'thinks it can fly,'* but *'then it likes once more/its earthly corner,'* he was attracted both to the sky and the earth, for, as he says in *Gitanjali*, *'Thou art the sky and thou art the nest as well.'* And in many of his poems, he expressed a deep empathy for the simple and ordinary rustic folks, who through the centuries have been labouring endlessly. In *Ora Kaj Kare* (They work) from *Arogya*, he writes:

... tane dar, dhorey thakay haal;
 ora mathay mathay
bij banay, paka dhan katey—
 ora kaj kare
 nagare prantare.

(...pulling oars, holding the plough, in field after field sowing seeds, reaping ripe paddy, they work in towns and corners.)

Again and again in poem after poem that touch our hearts—*Puratan Bhritya* (The Old Servant), *Dui Bigha Jami* (A Half-acre Plot)—Tagore wrote about the simplicity and the love and loyalty of rustic folks, who are easily cheated and abused. And in *Bansi* (Flute Music), he wrote of the '*torn umbrella*' and the '*royal parasol*' that merge and rise '*towards one heaven*' So that he says:

Akbar Badshar shangey
Haripada keranir kono bhed nai.

(There is no difference between Emperor Akbar and Haripada, the clerk.)

Underlying his unfailing romanticism, Tagore's humanism shines forth in several of his poems that are a magnificent blend of mysticism and reality.

Tagore's Short Stories

'To begin with I only wrote poetry—I didn't write stories. One day my father called me and said, 'I want you to take charge of the estates.' I was astonished: I was a poet, a scribbler—what did I know about such matters? But Father said, 'Never mind that—I want you to do it.' What could I do? Father had ordered me, so I had to go. Managing the *zamindari* gave me the opportunity to mix with various kinds of people, and this was how my story-writing began,' Tagore had said. And soon 'he showed himself a master from the very beginning.' He was the first writer to establish the short story as a literary *genre* in Bengali literature.

Tagore wrote several collections of stories and his most prolific period was in the 1890s, when he lived on the banks of the Padma river and in close contact with the countryside of Bengal and her peasants. This was also the time when Tagore made regular contributions to literary magazines, *Hitabadi, Sadhana, Bharati*, that were in vogue then and his readers made excited

Tagore: at about 45 years

demands for his stories. In his own words, his stories are 'full of the temperament of the rural people...' And 'their charming simplicity and deep—hearted affection make them much bigger than I am,' he said. Again and again he described the river Padma, both in its calm and majestic mood as well as in its destructive and terrifying state which Raicharan, the old servant, in *Khokababur Pratyabartan* (Little Master's Return) discovers, when it claims the life of his little ward:

'The rainy season came. The Padma began to swallow up gardens, villages and fields in great hungry gulps. Thickets and bushes disappeared from the sandbanks. The menacing gurgle of water was all around, and the splashing of crumbling banks; and swirling, rushing foam showed how fierce the river's current had become.'

Some of Tagore's short story collections are: *Chhoto Galpa, Vichitra Galpa, Katha Chatushtay, Galpa-Dasak, Galpa Chariti, Galpasalpa* (stories and poems). The four volumes of *Galpaguccha* (A Bunch of Stories) are collections of all his stories. Several anthologies of Tagore's stories in English were also published: *The Hungry Stones and Other Stories, Mashi and Other Stories, Stories from Tagore, Broken Ties and Other Stories*. Every reader of Tagore will have her/his favourites. Some of his unforgettable stories that come to mind are: *The Postmaster, Forbidden Entry Kabuliwallah, The Editor, The Hungry Stone, Skeleton,*

Wishes Granted, In the Middle of the Night, The Living and the Dead, Wealth Surrendered, The Gift of Sight, Little Master's Return, Profit and Loss, Punishment, etc. Tagore also had a penchant for the macabre and the supernatural and he wrote a number of fascinating ghost' stories like *Skeleton* and *The Hungry Stones*.

Like several of Tagore's plays, many of his stories—*Profit and Loss* (child-marriage and dowry system), *Punishment* (abject poverty) *Son-Sacrifice* (casteism),—expressed deep concern for the social inequalities of his time. But, it was the sense of the tragic and the ironic—the moments of anguished pain and sudden realization of the truth of life that he best portrayed in his stories. He delineated characters—Ratan, Kadambini, Jayakali

Still from the Satyajit Ray film Postmaster

Devi, Kabuliwallah, Banamali and a many others—with great psychological insight and depth, particularly the women, for whom he showed 'inexhaustible sympathy and admiration.' Ratan, the orphaned village-girl in the story *Postmaster* becomes deeply attached to the new postmaster, a Calcutta boy, from Ulapur, who begins to teach her to read a little bit every day, only because he is lonely. But one day, bored with village life, he asks for a transfer and leaves, offering the little girl some money, which Ratan refuses, saying, 'I beg you, Dadababu, I beg you - don't give me any money. Please, no one need bother about me.' These words echo the same hurt feelings of the Kabuliwallah, the trader from Afghanistan, in the story by the same name: 'Please, don't give me any money... Just as you have a daughter, so do I have one, in my own country. It is with her in mind that I came with a few raisins for your daughter: I didn't come to trade with you.' And in *Postmaster*, as Ratan's 'Dadababu,' sails away, leaving her weeping copiously and hoping that he would return, Tagore comments:

'O poor, unthinking human heart! Error will not go away, logic and reason are slow to penetrate. We cling with both arms to false hope, refusing to believe the weightiest proofs against it, embracing it with all our strength. In the end it escapes, ripping our veins and draining our heart's blood; until, regaining consciousness, we rush to fall into snares of delusion all over again.'

Still from the Satyajit Ray film Monihar

A number of Tagore's stories—*Postmaster, A Single Night, The Divide*—is about the bitter-sweet truth of life that is full of longings and hope as well as cold indifference and irony. And, it is the ordinary, the village girl or child, who attains immortality in his stories. Tagore's empathy with the common man and the deep insight into the heart and soul of his characters was an elemental feature of his creative genius as much as his romanticism. And so, when critics sometimes described his stories as unrealistic and over poeticized, he was hurt:

'I feel surprised when you say that my stories are over poetical... I would say there is no lack of realism in my stories. I wrote from what I saw, what I felt in my heart—my direct experience... Those who say that my stories are fanciful are wrong. Maybe one could say that in stories such as *Skeleton* or *The Hungry Stones* imagination predominates, but not completely even in those.'

Buddhadev Basu, the noted Bengali writer, said of his stories: 'All of Bengal can be found here. Not only facts, but her living soul: we feel her pulse as we turn the pages of *Galpaguccha*. Her changing seasons, the vital flow of her rivers, her plains, her bamboo-groves, her festival canopies and chariots; her cool, moist, richly fertile fragrance; her mischievous, noisy, lively boys and girls; her kind, skilled, intelligent women...'

The Novels of Tagore

Tagore wrote over a dozen novels between 1883.1934 starting with his first fiction *Bau-Thakuranir Hat*, (Daughter-in-law's Market) to his last novel *Char Adhyay* (Four Chapters). A number of these works were translated into English in Tagore's own lifetime: *Ghare-baire* as *The Home and the World*; *Nauka-dubi* as *The Wreck*; and *Gora* as *Gora*. His other novels are: *Rajarshi* (Royal Sage), *Chokher Bali* (Eyesore, translated as *Binodini*), *Chaturanga* (Four Colours), *Yogayog* (Cross Currents), *Sesher Kavita* (The Last Poem, translated as *Farewell, My Friend*), *Dui Bon* (Two Sisters), *Malancha* (Garden), and *Nasta Nir* (Broken Nest), which was made into an excellent film *Charulata* by Satyajit Ray.

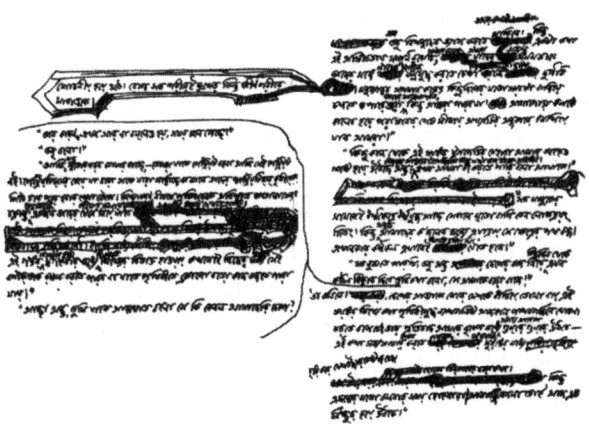

A folio form the manuscript of Chaar Adhyaye

Among all his novels *Gora* is considered by critics as Tagore's *magnum opus*, though *Sesher Kavita*, written in elegant prose and described as 'a love story written as if to end all love stories,' is also very popular. Written against the background of socio-religious problems of the 19th century, *Gora* deals with orthodoxy and explores the character of Indian nationalism with its rural—urban divide. Born of Irish parents, Gora is raised by Anandamayi after he is orphaned in the uprising of 1857. He knows nothing about his origins and though his foster-parents are liberal, he develops an orthodox mindset, which in the end gives way to genuine liberalism when he discovers the truth, including his own, about the innate unity of all cultures. In the end, he becomes Tagore's ideal 'universal man' as he says, 'I am an Indian today. In me there is no conflict with any community...'

Several of Tagore's novels deal with social issues and contradictions, and the disintegration of old values. In *Rajarshi*, he raised his voice against animal sacrifice, which was later adapted as a successful play *Visarjan*. And *Ghare-baire*, reviewed abroad, was described as 'a profoundly wise and beautiful book,' that 'succeeded in raising the social and political ferment of modern India to the high poetic plane with the least suppression of the truth, but force of vision.' This story of the political opportunist Sandip, Nikhil, the landlord, and his wife, Bimala, who comes under the spell of Sandip, is a testament of Tagore's 'insistent warning that wrong means must vitiate the end, however nobly conceived.'

Today, for some readers Tagore's stories may appear as 'period pieces,' reflecting outdated social mores, but his characters, in particular his women are memorable, for though they may live in a repressive society full of social disabilities, nevertheless they come out 'stronger than the men.' He explored again and again the theme of unfulfilled love and lack of opportunity for the development of woman's talents. As in many of his short stories, so in his fiction, his women characters live and breathe, revealing great psychological depth. Charulata in the novelette *Nasta Nir* and *Binodini*, the young widow, in *ChokherBali*, who refuses to accept restrictions, like the wife in the story *Strir Patra* (Wife's Letter) are among Tagore's best exploration of women's psyche. They come out as bold, assertive, desirous of freedom, who caused eyebrows to be raised among the orthodox of his time. The psychological stories of *Chokher Bali* and *Nasta Nir*, Krishna Kripalani says, 'laid the foundation of the modern novel in Indian literature.'

Tagore's Plays

Tagore wrote some forty-one plays, starting with *Valmiki Pratibha* (1881), a musical drama and later moved on to experiment with new dramatic modes, introducing songs and dances in several of his plays. A party of chorus singers, songs, music and dance became an essential feature of his *Giti-natya* (musical drama) and *Nritya-natya* (dance-drama). Often sitting on a stool in a corner, he sang on stage or played the part of the narrator.

The Jorasanko house had a private theatre and the literary club of the Tagores, which met regularly, commissioned Tagore to write plays for production. Often, the audience included well-known personalities like Bankim Chandra Chatterjee, the novelist. Sometimes, Tagore directed and acted in these plays along with his cousins and nephews, for instance acting as Valmiki in *Valmiki Pratibha* (Genius of Valmiki), as Raghupati in

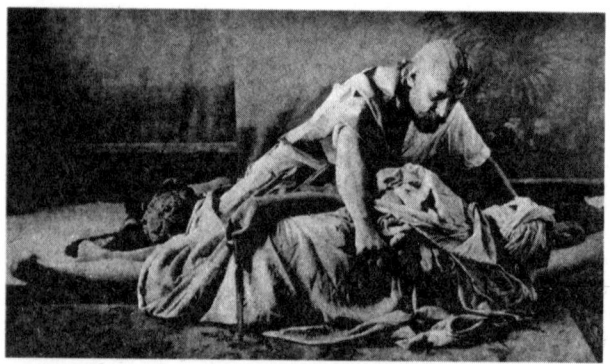

Tagore as Raghupati in his play Visarjan *and Arunendranath Tagore as Jaisingh, 1890*

Visarjan (Sacrifice) as a blind sage in *Kal Mrigaya* (Fateful Hunt), and in his sixties, as the king in *Tapati*. Later, many of his plays were staged at Santineketan, and in Calcutta.

Among some of Tagore's plays, to name a few, are: *Prakritir Pratisodh* (Nature's Revenge), *Mayar Khela* (Play of Illusions) which had all women characters, *Raja O Rani, Visarjan* (Sacrifice)' *Natir Puja* (Dancing-girl's Worship), *Phalguni* (Cycle of Spring), *Achalayatan* (Immovable), a satire on irrational habits and customs, *Muktadhara* (Free Current), *Raktakarabi* (Red Oleanders), and *Kaler Yatra*. While the last three plays questioned some of the tenets of modern civilization, *Prakritir Pratisodh*, an important early verse-drama, depicts how an untouchable girl makes a monk who has attained perfect detachment, realize that the great exist in the small. '...this has been the subject on which all my writings have dwelt—the joy of attaining the Infinite within the finite.' Some of his plays like *Syama* show an influence of Buddhist thought.

Often Tagore reworked his early works for adaptation for the stage, for instance, *Prayaschitta* (Atonement) was based on his early fiction *Bau-Thakuranir Haat*. His three most produced plays are: *Chitrangada, Syama*, and *Chandalika*. Other popular plays are: *Dakghar* (Post office), also staged in London, the comedy *Chirakumar Sabha* (Bachelor's Club), *Grihapravesh*. (Home - coming), and *Tasher-desh* (Country of Cards).

Essays and Letters of Tagore

Tagore's lectures, numerous essays, letters, and travel accounts form a substantial amount of his non-fiction writings. They cover an enormous range of topics from religious-philosophic subjects to aesthetics and education to subjects with more general appeal. Among his travel accounts are: *Europe Yatrir Dayari*; accounts of his first visits to England in two parts, 1891 and 1893; *Japan Yatri* travel to Japan; *Jatri*, travel accounts of journey to South America, Java; and *Pather Sanchay* (travel notes), which are essays written in 1912 on his visit to England and America and his impressions of the people he met—H G Wells, Rothenstein, Yeats, and others.

> There is a ~~sacred~~ passage in the Atharva Veda in
> which it is said that when his ^body was raised upwards he
> found also the oblique sides and all other directions in him
> It means that through the freedom of his bodily posture he finds himself
> in a large perspective which offers him not only individual
> facts and things but a great unity of view
> ~~through which he acquires~~ his own extension around himself. It also
> has its ~~inner~~ aspect, his mind ~~also has~~ ~~its own view~~ ~~enabling him to~~ ~~find his~~ reality across ~~the border~~ of his individual
> self. This denotes his spiritual freedom, his right of entrance
> into the heart of the all. ~~We have our~~ ~~us~~ vision of the
> eyes which relate ~~us~~ to the physical
> universe. ~~We also~~ ~~language~~ special faculty which helps
> ~~us~~ in finding ~~our~~ relationship with the supreme self
> of man. It is our imagination which in its fuller stage
> of development is peculiar to ~~us~~. It has its vision of
> wholeness which is not necessary for the biological purpose
> of physical survival but ~~for arousing~~ ~~in~~ us a sense of
> perfection which is our sense of immortality. For perfect

Rabindranath Tagore's erasures on a manuscript of The Religion of Man, *1930*

Among some of Tagore's collections of letters are: *Letters from Abroad* and *Letters to a Friend* addressed to his friend C F Andews, which include letters written between 1913–22; *Rashiar Chithi* (Letters from Russia), and *Chinnapatra*, (which was translated as *Glimpses*

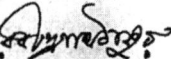

of Bengal). *Chinnapatra* is an interesting set of letters written to his niece, Indira Devi, between 1885 and 1895, the East Bengal years, and of which he said: 'They cover those years which were most productive for me and therefore they act like a footpath in my life history, unconsciously laid by the treading of my own thoughts.'

Among his important essays that give an insight into Tagore's mind are: *Sadhana: The Realization of Life*, Lectures in America between 1912—13, *Personality*,

52 • RABINDRANATH TAGORE

Rabindranath Tagore addressing girl students in Japan

Lectures delivered in America, 1917, *Nationalism*, Lectures delivered in Japan and the States, 1917, *Creative Unity*, essays and lectures on aesthetics, 1922, and *The Religion of Man Hibbert Lectures* at Oxford, 1930.

His early memoir *Jivansmriti*(1912), was translated by his nephew Surendranath Tagore in 1917 as *My Reminiscences*, while the account of his childhood *Chelebela*, written late in life, was translated by Marjorie Sykes as *My Boyhood Days*.

Tagore had his share of brickbats, hurt and disappointments; but let that be. His versatility and his fecundity are a marvel. None can fail to wonder at the man's limitless creative genius.

Dates of Selected Publications

EARLY WORKS

1873–75	Early verses and romantic narratives
1877	Begins regular contributions to *Bharati*.
1878	*Kavi-Kahini*, verse
1881	*Valmiki Pratibha*, musical drama
1882	*Sandhya Sangit*, verse; *Kal-Mrigaya*, musical drama
1883	*Prabhat Sangit*, verse; *Bau-Thakuranir Haat*, novel
1884	*Chabi O Gan*, verse; *Bhanusimha Thakurer Padavali*, poems and songs, *Prakritir Pratisodh*, verse drama
1885	*Rabichchhaya*, songs
1886	*Kadi O Kamal*, verse
1887	*Rajarshi*, novel
1888	*Samalochana*, essays; *Mayar Khela*, Musical drama
1889	*Raja O Rani*, first 5-act

IMPORTANT WORKS: 1890s and 1901–1929

1890	*Manasi*, verse; *Visarjan*, drama in verse (*Sacrifice and Other Plays* 1917, English translation)
1894	*Sonar Tari*, verse; *Chhoto Galpa* and *Vichitra Galpa* (1 & 11), stories
1895	*Galpa-Dasak*, stories
1896	*Chitra, Chaitali*, verses
1899	*Kanika*, 4 line verses
1900	*Katha, Kahini, Kalpana, Kshanika*, verses (*The Gardener*, 1913: authors translation of selections from *Kshanika, Kalpana, Sonar Tari*)
1901	*Naivedya*, verse
1902	*Nasta Nir*, novel
1903	*Chokher Bali*, novel; *Smaran,,* and *Sisu*, verse (*The Crescent Moon*, 1913, author's translatian of *Sisu*)
1906	*Kheya*, verse; *Naukadubi*, novel (*Love's Gift and Crossing* 1918, translations of selection from *Balaka, Kshanika, Kheya*)
1909	*Prayaschitta*, drama
1910	Bengali *Gitanjali*, songs and poems; *Gora*, novel, *Raja*, drama

1912	*Galpa chariti*, stories; *Galpaguccha* (A Bunch of Stories), English *Gitanjali* (Song Offerings), *Achalayatan* and *Dakghar*, drama; *Jibansmriti* (*My Reminiscences*), *Chhinnapatra*, letters
1913	*Sadhana*, essays
1914	*Gitimalya, Gitali*, songs, (Fruit-Gathering) *1916*, translation of selections from *Gitimalya, Gitali, Balaka*)
1916	*Balaka*, verse; *Ghara Baire*, novel; *Chaturanga*, novel
1917	*Personality, Nationalism,* essays; *My Reminiscences*, memoir, English translation
1918	*Palataka*, verse
1919	*Japan Yatri*, travel
1922	*Creative Unity*, essays; *Lipika*, prose-poems; *Sisu Bholanath*, verses; *Muktadhara*, drama
1924	Letters From Abroad
1925	*Grihapravesh*, drama; *Purabi*, verse
1926	*Natir Puja*, drama; *Chirakumar Sabha*, comedy; *Raktakarabi*, drama

1927	*Lekhan*, epigrams
1929	*Sesher Kavita* and *Yogayog*, novels; *Mahua*, verse

IMPORTANT WORKS: 1930–1941

1931	*The Religion of Man* (Hibbert Lectures at Oxford), *Russiar Chithi*, *The Child* (in English); *Sapmochan*, musical drama
1932	*Parisesh*, verse; *Punascha*, prose-poems; *Kaler Yatra*, drama
1933	*Dui Bon*, novel; *Chandalika* and *Tasher Desh*, drama
1934	*Malancha*, novel; *Char Adhyay*, novel
1935	*Bithika, Sesh Saptak*, verses
1936	*Syamali*, prose-poems; *Chitrangada*, dance-drama; *Patra-put*, prose-poems
1937	*Khapchhara*, nonsense rhymes
1938	*Prantik, Senjuti*, verses
1939	*Pather Sanchay*, essays; *Akash pradip*, verse; *Syama*, dance-drama

| 1940 | *Navajatak, Sanai*, verses; *Chhelebela* (translated as My Boyhood Days), memoir; *Rogashajyay*, verse |
| 1941 | *Arogya, Janmadine* verse, *Galpasalpa*, stories and poems |

(Several works of Tagore were published posthumously. For a complete bibliography, see Krishna Kripalani's biography.)

CHAPTER 3

TAGORE THE NOBEL LAUREATE

The English *Gitanjali*, the best known work of Tagore for which he was awarded the Nobel Prize for Literature in 1913, is a beautiful collection of hymns, full of 'music, mood and meditation.' Most of the compositions were written in Santineketan and at least one is recorded as written in Tindharia, a small township in the Himalaya, where the poet had gone on a visit. This was the period following the tragic series of bereavements that Tagore had suffered between 1902–1907, when he lost his. wife, daughter, father and his youngest son. The poet was in an intensely spiritual frame of mind, full of Divine consciousness, and he wrote:

That I want thee, only thee—let my heart repeat without end. All desires that distract me, day and night,

are false and empty to the core.
As the night keeps hidden in its gloom the petition
for light, even thus in the depth of my unconsciousness
rings the cry—'I want thee, only thee,'
(*XXXVIII*Gitanjali)

It was in such a state of mind, in total communion with the Lord that the profound lines of *Gitanjali* came to be penned:

He it is, the innermost one, who awakens my being
with his deep hidden touches.
He it is who puts his enchantment upon these eyes
and joyfully plays on the chords of my heart in varied
cadence of pleasure and pain.
(*LXXII*Gitanjali)

And:

In sorrow after sorrow it is his steps that press upon
my heart, and it is the golden touch of his feet that
makes my joy shine.
(*XLV*Gitanjaii)

Tagore described the *Gitanjali* songs as 'very intimately my own.' And he himself began a selected translation of the lyrics into English after a trip to England was cancelled due to ill health and he returned to Shelidah on the banks of his beloved Padma. As he explained, '...I had

60 • RABINDRANATH TAGORE

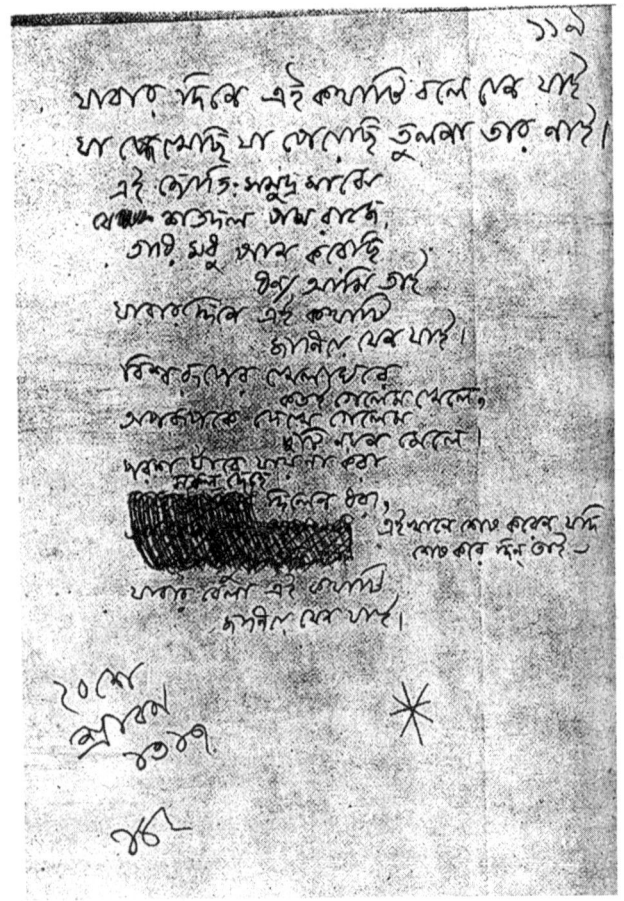

A folio from the original manuscript of Gitanjali *in Tagore's unique handwriting, which came to be known as 'Rabindrik' script*

not the energy to sit down and write anything new. So I took up the poems of *Gitanjali* and set myself to translate them one by one... I simply felt the urge to recapture through the medium of another language the feelings and sentiments which had created such a feast of joy within me in days gone by.' But he was rather apologetic for undertaking this task and he wrote, 'If anybody wrote an English note asking me to tea, I did not feel equal to answering it... that I have written in English seems to be a delusion.' Yet, it was this volume of translation that intoxicated his eminent western readers like Y B Yeats and Ezra Pound, the poets, and later drew the attention of the Nobel Prize Committee.

Sir William Rothenstein, the English painter, who was known to Abanindranath Tagore and Gaganendranath Tagore, the poet's artist nephews, visited Jorasanko in 1911, and had asked for the translation of some of Tagore's poems. When in England, Tagore showed Rothenstein the exercise-book containing his translations (which he continued to do on the ship to England)., with some diffidence.' But as Tagore said, 'I could hardly believe the opinion he (Rothenstein) expressed after going through it. He then made over the manuscript to Yeats. The story of what followed is known to you...' i.e. in his winning the Nobel Prize.

The West was enthralled by the intense sublimity of Tagore's poems with 'a deep and rare spiritual beauty.' Rothenstein, on reading the poems, said, 'Here was poetry of a new order, which seemed to me on a level with that of the great mystics.' Andrew Bradley, to whom I showed them agreed: 'It looks as though we have at last a great poet among us again.' Rothenstein sent word to Yeats, and when he failed to reply, he wrote to him again. Yeats asked for the poems, and when he read them, Rothenstein noted, 'his enthusiasm equaled mine.'

Yeats recorded his feelings in his Introduction to *Gitanjali*: 'I have carried the manuscript of these translations about with me for days, reading it in railway trains, or on the top of omnibuses and in

Rabindranath at the age of fifty by Sir William Rothenstein, the English painter, 1911

restaurants, and I have often had to close it lest some stranger would see how much it moved me. These lyrics—which are in the original, my Indian friends tell me are full of subtlety of rhythm, of untranslatable delicacies of colour, of metrical invention display in their thought a world I have dreamed of all my life long. The work of a supreme culture, they appear as much the growth of the common soil as the grass and the rushes.' Later, at a dinner in Tagore's honour, he described the happening as 'one of the great events of my artistic life.'

There is an interesting account in the poet's own words of his feelings at a reading of *Gitanjali* before its publication

Tagore being felicitated on winning the Nobel Prize at Santiniketan, November 1913

to an eminent gathering in England in 1912. Tagore was embarrassed but Yeats had insisted. 'So the arrangements were made, many luminaries arrived, *Gitanjali* was read. No one said a word—quietly they all listened and departed—no criticism, no accolades, not even a single word of encouragement!' In utter shame, the poet wished not to be and he became full of repentance and regret. But 'the next day the letters began to arrive, waves of them, each overwhelming in praise; letters came completely unexpectedly from every one of them.' And then Tagore said, '... I understood, they were all so deeply moved that evening that they had been unable to express themselves.'

Charles Freer Andrews, who became Tagore's lifelong friend and associate in Santineketan, who was present at the reading wrote: 'I want to be alone and think in silence of the wonder and glory of it all.' And Ezra Pound, noted, 'There is in him the stillness of nature... He is

Charles Freer Andrews

one with nature. And this is in sharp contrast with the Western mode, where man must be shown attempting to master nature if we are to have 'great drama'.'

There is this story of how this priceless manuscript was nearly lost. Tagore's son, Rathindranath, and his wife, Pratima Devi, had accompanied the poet on that trip to England. While travelling by tube from Charing Cross to Russell Square, Rathindranath, who was carrying his father's briefcase left it behind. Fortunately, the next morning, when his father asked for it, it was recovered from the Lost Property Office.

From England Tagore travelled to America, his first trip, when the news reached him that the Indian Society had published *Gitanjali* (1912) and that the book was very well received. Later it was published by Macmillan. In 1913 when he was in Santineketan, and 52 years of age, the news reached him that he had been awarded the Nobel Prize. Though one critic commented that the award was a proof that the British had civilized the Indians well enough to produce such good stuff, most newspapers were full of accolade for Tagore.

CHAPTER 4

TAGORE THE MUSICIAN AND THE PAINTER

'A strikingly handsome figure, dressed in a white *dhoti* and *chadar*... I felt an immediate attraction, and asked if I might draw him, for I discovered an inner charm as well as great physical beauty, which I tried to set down with my pencil...' so wrote Rothenstein, the painter, of Tagore.

Indeed, Tagore's handsome presence and his 'gentle voice' impressed all who met him. Aptly, Buddhadev Basu, the Bengali writer in a tribute to Tagore, described him as 'a phenomenon' and 'a force like nature's, expressing itself in literature.' And not only in literature but also in music and fine arts, Tagore was a master of melody and linear rhythm. Rightly, the Government of India named the building housing the three national academies of

Indian literature, music and drama, and fine arts—the Sahitya Akademi, the Sangeet-Natak Akademi and the Lalit-Kala Akademi—as the Rabindra Bhavan.

The Songs of Tagore

'My poems without their melodies are like butterflies without wings,' Tagore had stated. Perhaps, it may not be quite correct to rigidly separate his songs from his poems. For instance, Gitanjali, Gitimalya, and *Gitali* are as much poems as songs and he set to music a number of his poems. But he also wrote over two thousand songs, short and simple compositions, that were set immediately to tune. *Rabichhaya* was his first' collection of songs.

Tagore at Oxford in 1930

'It is an old habit of mine, as you know, that when the air strikes my bones, they tend to respond in music...' Tagore said and giving melody to words was for him a passion. He had grown up in an atmosphere filled with the sound of music of organ, piano, violin and *Brahmo Sangit*, and *jalsas* or musical evenings were frequently held at Jorasanko. Celebrated musicians came to stay with the family. And he was familiar with the songs and tunes of the boatmen and Bauls, the wandering minstrels of Bengal, so that his music drew from classical, folk and western traditions.

Sarojini Naidu, the poetess, described Tagore's music 'as fresh as the first flowers of springtime and as enchanting as the music of moonlit stream,' and said his songs would remain for generation after generation. And William Radice, Tagore scholar, noted: 'Tagoreexpressed his romantic and religious perception most profoundly in his songs: the essential harmony and beauty of the universe…was best conveyed through music…' A characteristic devotional strain of his music goes:

Shimar maje ashim tumi
bajao apon shur,
Amar modhe tomar prakash tai toe etho madhur.

(Thou, the infinite within the finite, play your tune. Your light is within me, so my melody is sweet.)

Tagore described music as reciprocal. In *Gan-bhango* (Broken Song), he writes: '*The singer alone does not make a song, there has to be someone who hears.*' And; '*Wjhere*

there is no love, where listeners are dumb, there never can. be song,' Indeed, it is in Tagore's imperishable songs, *Rabindra Sangit*, an essential element of Bengali culture, that he and his people have the closest bond. During Puja festivities, *pandals* reverberate with his songs from his musical plays and his dance-dramas are often staged on these occasions. And in every Bengali household the sound of music f very often is *Rabindra Sangit* rendered by noted artistes like Hemant Kumar, Debabrata Biswas, and Suchitra Mitra and others:

Akash bhora, surjo tara
Bisho bhara pran,
Tahari majkhane ami paechi mor sthan
Bishoy tai jage amar gan

(The sky full of stars; the universe full of life. Amidst these I have found my place and so my song rises in the whole universe.)

Tagore himself arranged his songs in his collection *Geetobitan* under different topics: *Puja* (Devotion), *Swadesh* (My Country), *Prem* (Love), *Prakriti* (Nature), *Giti-Natya*, and *Nritya Natya* (Musical Dance and Dance-Drama). The songs of the seasons are grouped under the six seasons of the country: *Grishma* (summer), *Barsha* (monsoon), *Sharad* (autumn), *Sith* (winter), and *Basanta* (spring). The famous songs: O, *amar desher mati tomar, pore thekai matha* (O, my country I bow my head to your land) and *Jodi tor dak shune kau na ashe tobe ekla cholo re* (If no one comes hearing your call, then walk alone) are patriotic songs from *Swadesh*, which also includes *Janaganamana*, India's national anthem. His song *Our Golden Bengal* was adapted as the national anthem of Bangladesh.

Tagore was often asked to write songs and he wrote *Amra milechi maayer dake* (We've united at the call of our Mother) for the Indian National Congress in 1886 and when Gandhi broke his fast-unto-death in 1932 at Poona, he sang a song to mark that occasion.

Tagore's Drawing and Paintings

Tagore said that from his early days 'his eyes were hungry for the world of forms.' And with no formal training in fine arts, he began painting at the ripe age of 67 and exhibiting his unique art in the world's capitals. His art—about 2,500 drawings and paintings—had their origin in his erasures—the patterned scratches blotting out unwanted words and lines in the manuscripts of his poems that he casually drew but which grew into images impregnated with life. Victoria Ocampo, Tagore's admirer, with whom he stayed as a guest in Buenos Aires while convalescing and who had watched him making the doodles in his *Purabi* poems in 1924, described them as 'lines that suddenly jumped into life out of this play; prehistoric monsters, birds, faces appeared.'

In 1930 Tagore took 400 paintings with him to Europe when he visited England via France to deliver the Oxford Hibbert Lectures. He also visited Germany, Russia, Switzerland and the United States. And an exhibition of his art was held in Paris, Birmingham, Berlin, Moscow, and New York. Describing these works, the curator of the art gallery in Moscow noted, '...the more we acquaint ourselves with his paintings, the more we are struck.' While Ananda Coomaraswamy, the art-historian, described his work as 'genuine examples of modern primitive art.' For unlike Tagore's poems that celebrated the beautiful, his art expressed the grotesque. His erasures and his early paintings are full of strange creatures, goggle-eyed birds, beaked-heads imbued with qualities of primitive art that, critics say, the poet may have been familiar with. During his numerous travels abroad, it is likely he became acquainted with European and primitive art when he visited museums and art galleries. However, Tagore's unpremeditated art is generally believed to be born of the dark unconscious, unlike his poems which can be traced back to conscious thought.

After the doodles phase, Tagore largely did single images mostly in ink and 'Sometimes the black ink began to flow like the river Padma in the cold weather, interspersed with many sandy islands and rivulets, and, at other times it coursed down like the Ganges at Hoogly.' Towards 1930, he began using colour—pencils and crayons—applied sometimes with a blade. And in the last phase, Tagore painted several heads with grimacing expressions; dark, mysterious female figures reflecting deep emotions; figures suggesting actions; three self-portraits; flowers and landscapes full of atmosphere. His best work includes his ink works, expressionistic heads and landscapes with no realistic detail.

Indeed, Tagore's vast and varied works, his universalism, his humanism, speak of his multifaceted genius and the richness of his spirit. Mahatma Gandhi called him 'the greatest poet of the age.' Dr S Radhakrishnan, the savant, described him as 'the greatest figure of the modern Indian Renaissance.' And Pandit Nehru noted, 'I have no doubt in my mind that the two biggest I have had the privilege of meeting have been Gandhi and Tagore.'

FROM THE *GITANJALI*

*Life of my life, I shall ever try to keep my body pure,
knowing that thy living touch is upon all my limbs.
I shall ever try to keep all untruths out from my
thoughts, knowing that thou art that truth which has
kindled the light of reason in my mind.
I shall ever try to drive all evils away from my heart
and keep my love in flower, knowing that thou hast
thy seat in the inmost shrine of my heart.
And it shall be my endeavour to reveal thee in my
actions, knowing it is thy power gives me strength to act.*

*Have you not heard his silent steps? He comes, comes,
ever comes.*

*Every moment and every age, every day and every
night he comes, comes, ever comes.*

Many a song have I sung in many a mood of mind,

Rabindranath Tagore during the Gitanjali *period*

but all their notes have always proclaimed, 'He comes, comes, ever comes.'

In the, fragrant days of sunny April through the forest path he comes, comes, ever comes.

In the rainy gloom of July nights on the thundering chariot of clouds he comes, comes, ever comes.

In sorrow after sorrow it is his steps that press upon my heart, and it is the golden touch of his feet that makes my joy to shine.

Thou hast made me endless, such is thy pleasures. This frail vessel thou emptiest again and again, and fillest it ever with fresh life.

This little flute of a reed thou hast carried over hills and dales, and hast breathed through it melodies eternally new.

At the immortal touch of thy hands my little heart loses its limits in joy and gives birth to utterances ineffable.

They infinite gifts come to me only on these very small hands of mine. Ages pass, and still thou pourest, and still there is room to fill.

Where the mind is without fear and the bead is held high;
   Where knowledge is free;
   Where the world has not been broken up into fragments by narrow domestic walls;

Where words come out from the depth of truth;
Where tireless striving stretches its arms towards
perfection;
Where the clear stream of reason has not lost its way
into the dreary desert sand of dead habit;
Where the mind is led forward by thee into ever-
widening thought and action—
Into that heaven of freedom, my Father, let my country
awake.

You came down from your throne and stood at my cottage
door.
I was singing all alone in a corner, and the melody caught
your ear. You came down and stood at my cottage door.
Master are many in your hall, and songs are sung
there at all hours. But the simple carol of this novice
struck at your love. One plaintive little strain mingled
with the great music of the world, and with a flower
for a prize you came down and stopped at my cottage door.

Rabindranath Tagore

CHRONOLOGY

1861	7th May, Birth of Tagore in Calcutta
1873	Trip to the Himalay as with his father; first visit to Santineketan
1875	Leaves school, Mother passes away
1877	He started contributing regularly in *Bharati*, the literary magazine of the Tagore family
1879	Admitted to University College, London. Returns after a year without completing studies
1882	His *Sandhya Sangeet* (Evening Songs) praised by Bankim Chandra Chatterji
1883	He is married to Mrinalini Devi
1884	His sister-in-law Kadambari Devi commits suicide

1890	He is put in charge of his family estates. Starts to write for *Sadhana*, a new family magazine. Second visit to England
1901	School at Santineketan founded
1902	His wife passes away
1905	His father dies. Leads protest against the partition of Bengal
1910	Bengali *Gitanjali* is published
1912	English *Gitanjali* published. Third trip to England and first to the USA
1913	Nobel Prize for Literature. University of Calcutta confers Doctor of Letters
1914	C F Andrews, Tagore's staunch friend, joins Santineketan
1915	Awarded Knighthood. First meeting with Gandhi at Santineketan
1916	Visits Japan and the USA, lectures on *Nationalism* and *Personality*
1919	Returns Knighthood
1920–21	Visits England, Europe and America. Detaches himself from Swaraj campaign. Visva-Bharati University inaugurated
1924	Travels to China and Japan. Sails to South America

1926	Tours Europe. Meets Romain Rolland and Einstein in Europe
1927	Tours Southeast Asia
1928	Starts Painting
1929	Visits Canada, Japan, Saigon
1930	Hibbert Lectures (*The Religion of Man*) at Oxford. Exhibition of his paintings in Paris, Birmingham, London and several other European capitals, also in New York. Visits Russia
1932	Visits Iran and Iraq
1934–36	Third visit to Sri Lanka with dance-troupe from Santineketan
1937	Delivers Convocation Address, Calcutta University, in Bengali, he falls ill
1940	Oxford University confers Doctorate on Tagore, C F Andrews dies
1941	Tagore passes away in Calcutta

BIBLIOGRAPHY

Rabindranath Tagore: A Biography
by Krishna Kripalani. Visva-Bharati

Life of Tagore
by Probhat Kumar Mukherji.
Translated by Sisirkumar Ghosh.
Indian Book Company

The Paintings of three Tagores: Abanindranath, Gaganendranath and Rabindranath
by Ratan Parimoo.
Published by MS University, Baroda

Collected Poems and Plays. Rabindranath Tagore
Macmillian

Rabindranath Tagore, Selected Short Stories
translated by William Radice. Penguin Books

The Art of Rabindranath Tagore
by Andrew Robinson. Rupa Publications India Pvt. Ltd.